Walks in the

France and Spain

The Basque country is a wonderful area for mountain walking, with summits and corresponding views accessible to the ordinary walker, unlike in the high Pyrenees. It is a great area to walk in all year round.

25 walks are described.

Walks

1 Pasaia - San Sebastian (Donostia) 7
2 Jaizkibel 9
3 Peñas de Aia 11
4 Corniche Coastal path 14
5 Mendaur 16
6 Mandale 18
7 La Rhune 20
8 Guéthary to St Jean de Luz 23
9 Col des Trois Fontaines 26
10 Atxuria 29
11 Alcurrunz 31
12 Mondarrain 34
13 Ursuya 36
14 Gorospil Cirque 38
15 Baigora 40
16 Ichusi 42
17 Mt Larla Mining circuit 44
18 Crêtes d'Iparla from Urdos 46
19 Iparla from Ispeguey 48
20 Hautza 51
21 Harguibel 53
22 Monhoa 55
23 Occabe 57
24 Escaliers – Arthanolatze 60
25 Pic d'Orhy 62

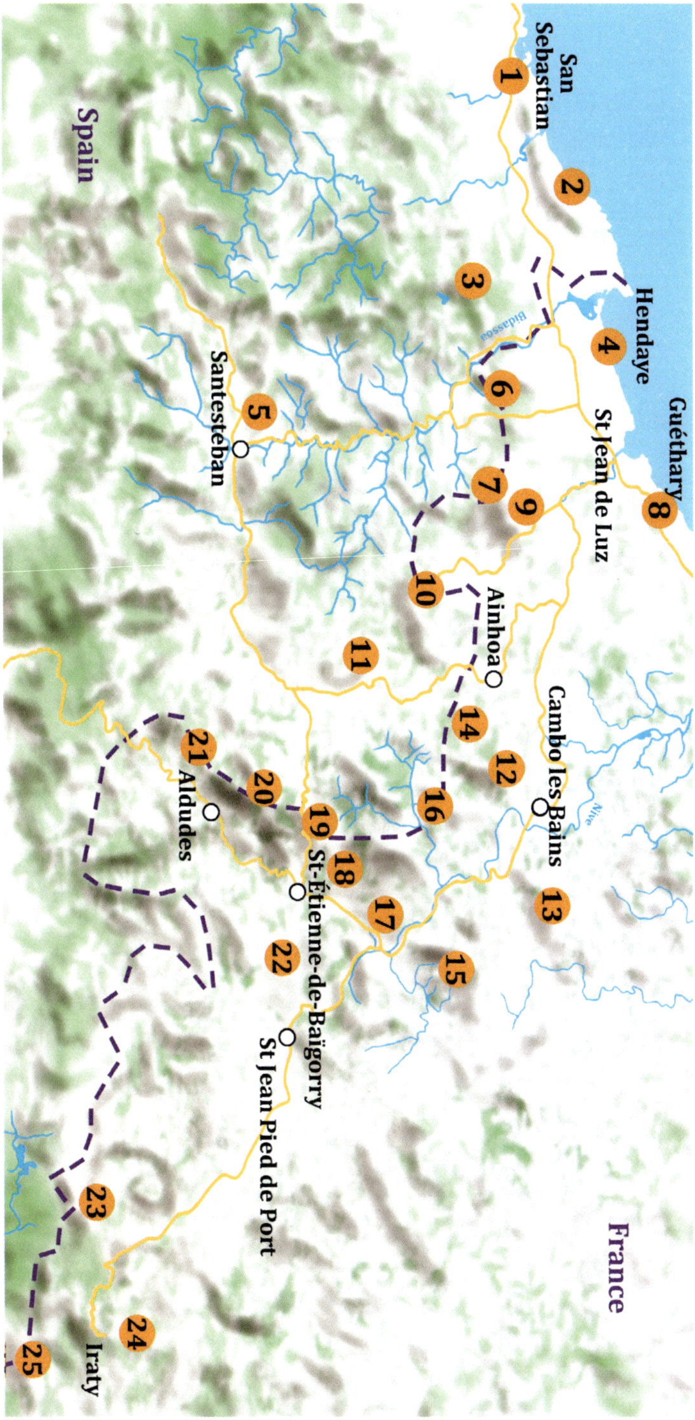
San Sebastian
1
2
Hendaye
4
3
Bidassoa
6
Guéthary
8
St Jean de Luz
9
7
5
Santestéban
10
Ainhoa
11
Cambo les Bains
Nive
13
12
14
16
19
21
20
Aldudes
18
17
St-Étienne-de-Baïgorry
22
15
St Jean Pied de Port
23
24
25
Iraty
France
Spain

Introduction

The Basque country comprises 7 provinces, 4 in Spain and 3 in France. The walks in this book are in the northern part of this mountainous region, and many are near or on the international frontier. Most walks are in the mountains though there are a few coastal walks. They tend to be between 3 and 5 hours long and have less than 1000m of ascent. There is a rich tradition of walking in the Basque country, with the long distance Pyrenean routes GR10, GR11 and Pyrenean Haute Route crossing the region, as well as the Way of St James' French and Northern routes.

When to go
The lower mountains near the coast are accessible all year round. When snowfalls occur they usually clear within a few days. Further inland, from Mt Iparla east, the snow stays longer. On hot days in the summer, an early start allows the walker to enjoy the cooler breeze on the ridges.

Equipment
Many of the routes listed involve walking in places that are not much frequented so parties should come prepared.
Bring a map and a compass or GPS, waterproof clothing and a litre of water per person. The Basque Country is oceanic as well as mountainous and sudden changes of weather do occur. The warm weather brought by the southern wind will often be followed by a period of instability. Water can usually be found but there is grazing by horses and sheep on most mountains and water should be sterilised if not from a spring.

History
The region is very rich in evidence of prehistoric human settlement. Walkers will find large numbers of iron age stone circles, as well as dolmens and menhirs. Most were constructed in the first millennium BC. More modern military structures dating from the Napoleonic, Carlist or World wars are also to be seen.

Wildlife
An ancient race of pony, the *Pottok*, lives in semi-liberty on the mountains. The Basque mountains are home to large numbers of different birds or prey, especially vultures which you are certain to see. In the autumn the area is part of an important bird migration route from Northern Europe to Africa. Walkers should keep an eye out for snakes.

Safety
In France and Spain the emergency mountain rescue number is 112.

Maps
Nearly all walks are covered by the two IGN 1/50,000 maps:
Pays Basque ouest; Pays Basque est
The corresponding IGN 1/25,000 maps are also useful:
Hendaye/St-Jean-De-Luz; Cambo-Les-Bains;
Saint-Jean-Pied-De-Port; Forêt d'Iraty Pic d'Orhy

GPS Maps
TOPO *France PRO – Montagne*

TOPO *Alpina Espana - Pirineo Aragones y Navarro*

Spelling
Many of the Basque place names used in this guide can be spelt differently in French and Spanish maps and on signposts. This guide uses the spelling of the IGN map series.

Navigation
Many of the walks have waymarks.

Glossary
Bergerie – a building in high country used by pastoralists
Col - a low point on a ridge
Poudding – a rock form made up of sand and pebbles
Venta – a shop or bar on the Spanish side of the border
Cromlech – used in France and Spain to mean stone circle
Dolmen – burial chamber
Menhir – standing stone
Fronton – a place to play Pelota, usually in the centre of the village
Pelota – Basque ball game

1. Pasaia - San Sebastian (Donostia)

A delightful cliff top walk through lush vegetation and with fine views. It is possible to walk just one way and return by public transport or taxi.
2 hours 45', 250m of ascent

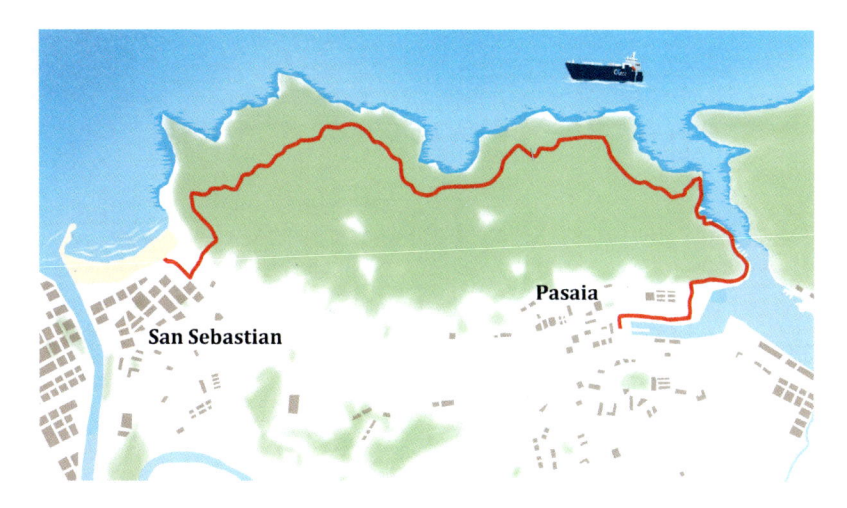

ACCESS: Park near the port at Pasaia.

WALK
Walk towards the narrow entrance of the harbour. After 10' pass the ferry going across the river to Pasajes, a nice place to have lunch. Continue along the river passing the *Albaola* ship-building museum before reaching the lighthouse at the entrance of the estuary.

25' Steps - Climb the steps steeply up the cliff up to a road. Turn right (N) on the road leading to a turreted lighthouse on a promontory.

50' Lighthouse - Just before the lighthouse turn left onto the coastal path near a panel about the geology of the sandstone formations on the coast. Follow the red/white waymarks of the GR121 (tour of Guipizkoa) which you follow today. (The yellow waymarks indicate the Way of St James northern route.)

1 hr, Water source and aqueduct, known as the *'fuente del Ingles'* after the English troops who were stationed here during the siege of San Sebastian in 1813. The aqueducts were used to supply San Sebastian with drinking water.

1hr 20' - Stay right at a junction where the way of St James goes left. Pass another water source and then cross a road.

2hrs, Viewpoint - The path zigzags up above the highest section of cliffs (177m)

2hrs, 15' - Join a track, then descend through woods with views over the city. Turn right onto a concrete path and then steps. At a road turn right and go down towards the beach (playa de Gros). Follow the sea front and cross the river on a bridge.

2hrs, 45' San Sebastian

If starting the walk from San Sebastian you need to go to playa de Gros and then turn right up 'Zemoriya' street.

2. Jaizkibel

A long whaleback ridge with views of the ocean and the bay of Txingudi.
2 hours 30', 400m ascent

ACCESS: Start at the monastery of Guadeloupe (192m, *0595510 – 4802211)*, signposted from the roundabout outside the airport at Hondarribia.

WALK
Head WSW up the concrete path following the red and white of the GR121 (Tour of Guipizkoa). After 5' climb steeply SW up the ridge, through a gate and up to a ruined tower.

30' Tower dating from the last Carlist war (1872-76) 380m, survey marker. Continue along the crest of the ridge past two dolmens and a standing stone to a second tower.

60' Carlist tower, 412m, car park with panoramic viewpoint. Go through a style and up the ridge towards the summit.

90' Jaizkibel 547m summit with antennae. Views along coast W to San Sebastian and beyond. Return by the same route. As you approach the monastery notice the impressive Guadeloupe Fort just beyond.

2hrs, 30' Monastery of Guadeloupe.

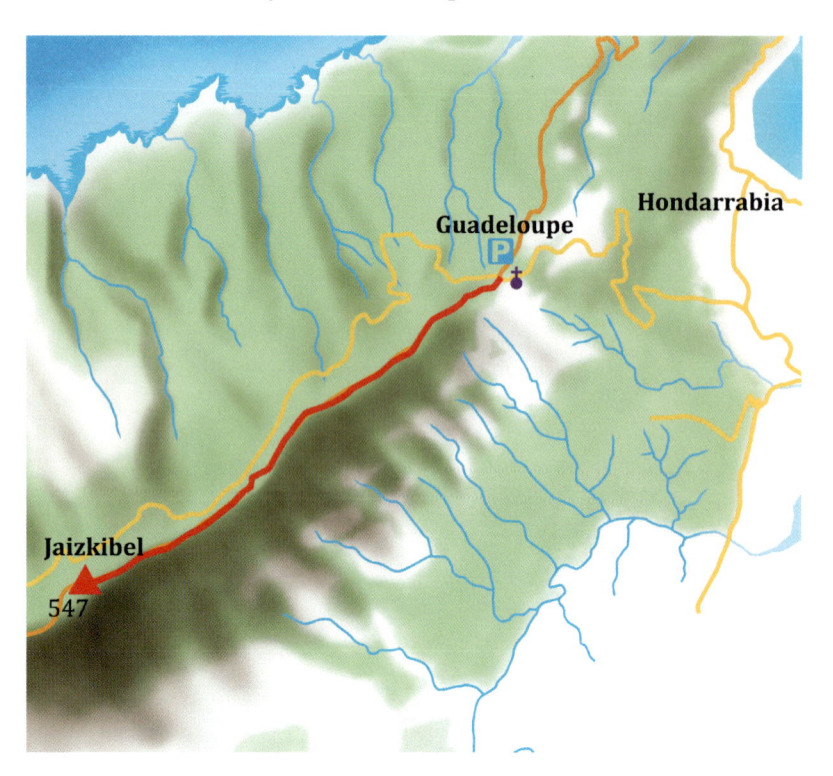

The Carlist wars were a series of civil wars that took place in Spain in the 19th century pitting different royalists against liberals and later republicans.

3. Peñas de Aia

A granite ridge with three summits, the first being easily accessible in less than an hour while the rest of the ridge provides a stunning airy scramble. Also known as the 'Trois Couronnes' *this mountain was an important mining area up until the beginning of the 20th century.*

3 hours, 550m of ascent. 2 hours if just going to first summit

ACCESS: When coming from France, cross the border on the N10 at Behobia, and turn right towards Irun. After 1.7km go round the roundabout and back the way you came. After 50m take the first right, signed *'Peñas de Aia'*. The road goes under the motorway, up to a *col* with picnic tables, and past the ruins of the *'Castillo del Ingles'* before arriving at a car park on the left, near a pylon. This is the Col d'Exurretxe.

WALK

Col d'Exurretxe 490m - Take the path up through the forest to the left of the pylon. After 10' turn right up the hill at a signpost and then follow the fence line. Go up through fir and beech trees and past a wartime pillbox built as part of a defensive network along the border to prevent an invasion from the north. The path turns left and two long zigzags take you to the summit ridge which is straddled by a cave (760m). The path crosses over to the western side of the ridge where the cave contains a water source.

45' - Cross back to the eastern side of the ridge. The main path skirts under the first summit but it is a short clamber up the slope to enjoy the fine views from the top of Irumugarieta.

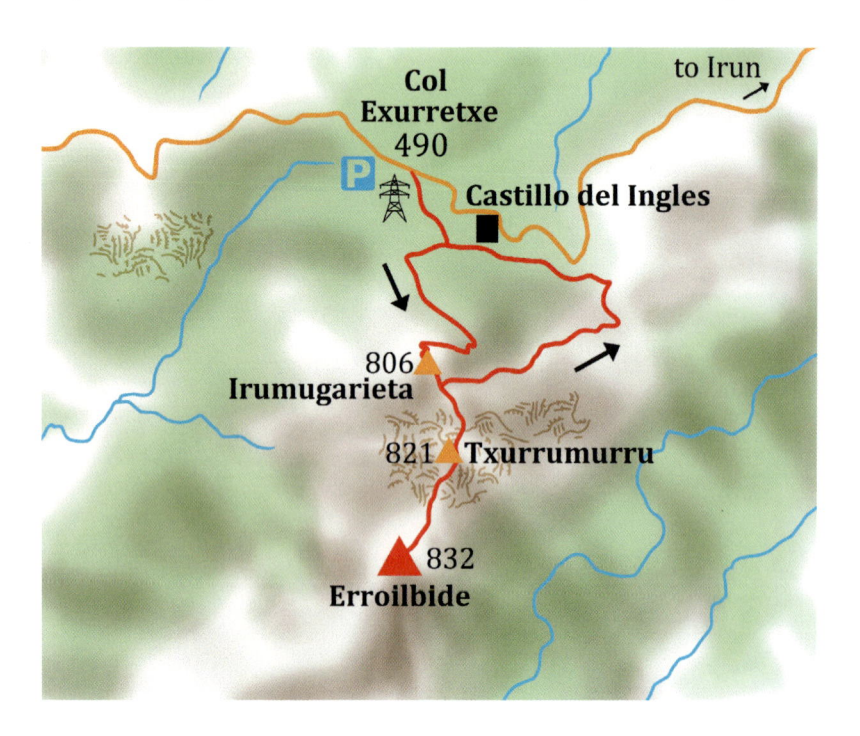

55' Irumugarieta, 806m. - Go back down to the path and continue towards the next summit. Just after a cleft in the rock an awkward step is required to cross a gully. Leave the path at the next high point to scramble up rocks and then a steep eroded path to the summit of Txurrumurra.

1hr 10', Txurrumurra 826m, statue of bird. Return the same way to rejoin the ridge path which then drops sharply. At 740m climb right over rocks following red marks. It is easy scrambling to start with though a bit exposed. The final awkward traverse down to the *col* is protected by a large ring. A rope should be used. Follow the ridge, with several sections that require scrambling, to the summit of Erroilbilde.

1 hr 45' Erroilbilde 836m - Return along the ridge until below the northern summit. Drop down east on a path through forest and then an open grassy slope followed by more forest until the slope levels off and you encounter a path and signpost. Turn left towards 'Arestegieta'. After a few hundred metres turn left at a junction. This is the GR121 (tour of Guipizkoa).

2hrs, 15' Turn left and follow the white/red/yellow waymarks. Go over an old mining railway viaduct, built by the British *Bidasoa Iron Company* in the late 19th century to transport iron down to the coast. Pass the ruins of the mining office and accommodation at *Castillo del Ingles* (2hrs, 40') and then turn left and up through the woods and back to the Col d'Exurretxe.

3hrs - Col d'Exurretxe.

4. Corniche Coastal path

The Corniche is the beautiful rocky coastline between St Jean de Luz and Hendaye.
1 hour 30'

ACCESS: It is possible to walk all the way along the coastal path from St Jean de Luz to Hendaye but the eastern section runs close to the road so it is better to start walking half way along. As you come along the road from St Jean de Luz you will see a large building with a tidal pool. This was formerly a hotel called 'Haizabia' and is now a holiday centre for railway workers. It is opposite the entrance to '*Pierre et Vacances*'. There are a few places to park in front of the old hotel.

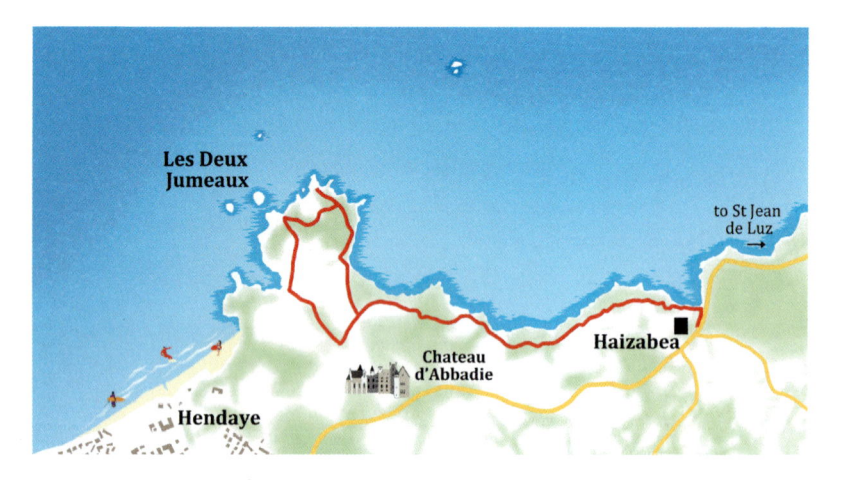

WALK
Turn right just before the building by a sign '*Sentier du Littoral*'. Note the yellow waymarks that will guide you today. Walk down to the coast and turn left and past the tidal pool and then up steps to the cliff top path.

10' - Pass the ***'Maison de la Corniche Basque'*** which has information about the geology and wildlife of the area. Soon after, you enter the Abbadie estate. Continue on the well-made path that undulates across open country with sea views, and through woodland. At a junction, turn right towards the sea and then left, following a sign to '*Larretxea*'

30' - At another junction, turn right towards the sea. Look out for orchids and other wild flowers in the meadows. A number of paths lead off to the right. These take you to viewpoints on the cliff top, one of which has a WWII blockhouse with new age symbols, another has a blockhouse and a great view of the two offshore rocks known as the '*Jumeaux*' (twins) as well as of Hendaye beach and Spain beyond. Head back inland towards the chateau.

55' - At a junction walk up through meadows and then woods towards the chateau. The chateau was built by Antoine d'Abbadie, an extraordinary polymath and astronomer who wrote the first Basque grammar and also mapped parts of Ethiopia. The chateau is well worth a visit, though you need to access it from the main road.

60' - Turn left at a junction, and at the end of a meadow go straight on, you are back on the path you came on.

1hr 30' - Return to the start

5. Mendaur

A fine summit in Navarre, with a hermitage.
450m of ascent, 2 hours 45'

ACCESS: Start from the village of Aurtitz, on the road from Santesteban to Leitza. It is possible to extend the walk by starting from the village following red/white waymarks but you can drive 500m up to the Mendaur reservoir on a dirt road and the walk is described from there. Coming from Santesteban, turn right just after Aurtitz on the road marked 'Mendaur', this soon becomes concrete and later dirt. Park near the reservoir.

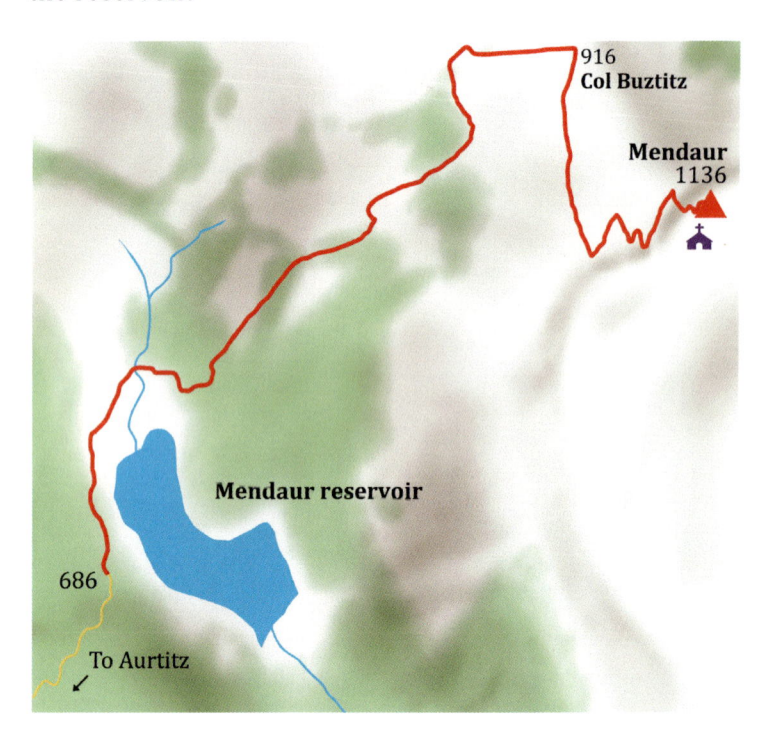

WALK

Mendaur reservoir 684m - Walk round the head of the reservoir past a concrete wall following the red/white waymarks which will guide you today. Stay right at a junction, pass some picnic tables and a stream and then climb NE through woods going towards the *col* to the left of Mendaur.

1hr Col Buztitz 916m, standing menhir (recently erected) zigzag E up the ridge at first before tracking right and approaching the summit from the SW through blocks of *poudding* and then up some steps.

1hr 30' Mendaur 1136m, *0604128 4778874* The Hermitage of the Holy Trinity, built in 1693, was ordered to be demolished by a bishop as it was used by bandits in 1781, but was reprieved in the resultant court case. Descend the same way in 1 hr 15'

2 hrs 45' – Reservoir

6. Mandale

A short walk with fine mountain scenery and views of the coast. You will pass stone circles and a Napoleonic redoubt.
1 hour 30', 200m of ascent

ACCESS: Drive to the Col d'Ibardin, pass a lot of Spanish supermarkets and park at the highest *venta*, Venta Elizalde, with a view down to St Jean de Luz and the coast.

WALK
Take the path going W up the ridge marked with the red and white waymarks of the GR10. After a short while the path joins a dirt road which winds SW up and round the flank of the mountain eventually levelling off with a pine forest on your right. At the end of the dirt road (25') continue along the path that follows the contour SW round the side of the mountain with a view down to the reservoir below and opening views over the bay of Txingudi and the Peñas de Aia in Spain.

35' - Leave the GR when it turns to follow the ridge NW towards Hendaye and follow the trail that climbs up SE to the summit ridge of the Mandele. Turn SW to take the view from the subsidiary summit; (frontier stone 8, 514m, 45'). Retrace your steps back up the ridge to the main summit.

1hr 5' Mandale , frontier stone 9. The summit is circled by a defensive fortification used by the Napoleonic army at the battle of the Rhune in 1813.
Follow the ridge E which descends past a pine forest on your right and levels off at a clearing with some stone circles.

1hr 15' stone circles. The path threads its way through some rocks and then down the increasingly steep ridge back to the start where refreshments are available.

1hr 30' Venta Elizalde

Stone circle

7. La Rhune

Visible from all along the coast the Rhune is an outstanding viewpoint whose summit is only somewhat marred by a huge antenna and three Spanish ventas providing refreshments to the many tourists who go up in the elegant wooden carriages of the rack railway. The route described here is a mountain cirque starting at the Gîte in Olhete.

4 hours 30', 900m of ascent

ACCESS: Leave the D44 west of Ascain at the first of the two roads opposite the Hotel Trabenea, signed 'La Rhune'. After 500m the road ends at a car park in the forest.

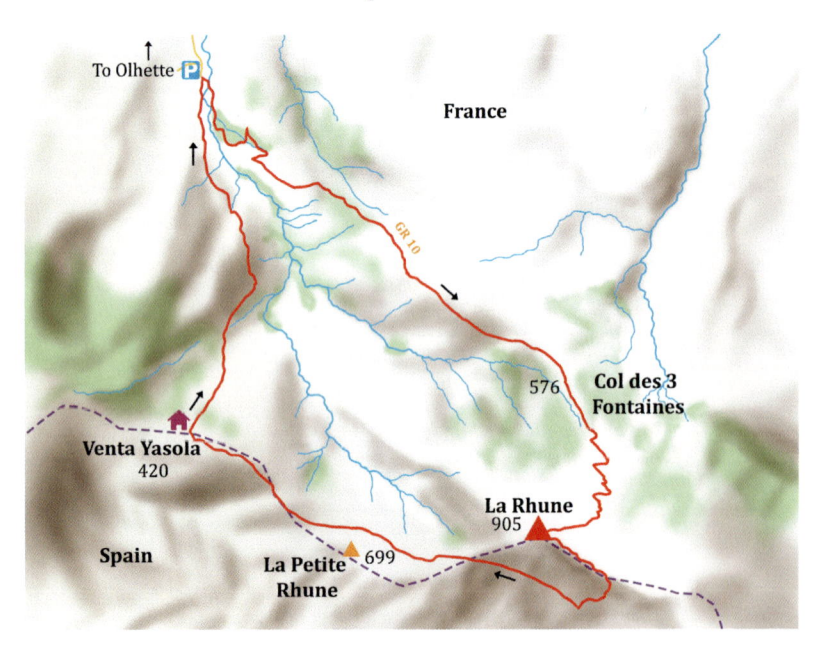

WALK

Walk up the path at the end of the car park by the large 'Depart' sign. This is the GR10 which you follow as far as the *'Col des Trois Fontaines'*. Follow the red and white waymarks along the wide path up through deciduous forest. After 15' the path emerges from the forest and continues south along the side of the ridge.

35' Col, continue up the crest of the ridge and after 10' veer right at a junction to flank the ridge again.

1 hr 25' Col des Trois Fontaines 563m - Leave the GR and take the obvious path up SW between trees towards the summit of the Rhune. Follow the yellow marks or downward green arrows as you climb steadily up the stony terrain. Cross the railway track a few metres before the summit.

2hrs, 15' La Rhune 905m Railway station, antenna and monument to the ascension of Empress Eugenie in 1859. Three *ventas* provide refreshments, the lowest one is open for walkers most of the year. Go down SE on the dirt road which soon turns back to the west and passes under the summit.

2hrs, 45m' Col de Zizkuitz, 665m, frontier stone 23. Turn right off the road, go over the *col* and then veer left (NW) through mature beech trees.

2hrs, 55' Rock carvings in memory of the patriot Maurice Abeberry on your left, then the path skirts under the summit of the Petite Rhune until you come to a ridge which you follow down to a *col* where you veer left along the edge of a conifer plantation. The path joins another and then drops steeply (slippery if wet) to the *Venta Yasola*.

3hrs, 30', Venta Yasola, 420m, refreshments, (Tel: 0034609515860, worth booking if you expect lunch) the path goes down north towards Biarritz and the coast.

4hrs, Col de Deskargahandia 274m several paths meet, take the right hand path with the red/white GR waymarks. Stay high when the path splits.

4hrs, 30' Gite de Olhette, which provides accommodation for long distance walkers. Cross the bridge over the river back to the car park.

Empress Eugenie, the wife of Napoleon III, climbed the Rhune in 1859. The party travelled to and from Biarritz by horse carriage and then on the back of mules up the mountain, stopping for a large lunch half-way up. This was followed by dancing and an exhibition match of pelota and the party arrived on the summit at dusk. The monument to this event originally had a bronze eagle on the top but this was removed in 1940, to be used for German munitions.

8. Guéthary to St Jean de Luz

Walk along the coastal path past beaches, on cliff top paths and small roads with views up and down the coast from Biarritz to Spain. Walkers can take the train from St Jean de Luz to Guéthary and walk back, or vice versa.
2 hours 45' each way

ACCESS: Start in Guéthary, a village popular with surfers.

WALK
Cross the railway bridge near the station and go down through the port to the sea front and pass some fish restaurants. At the end of the tarmac, note the yellow waymarks you will follow today and go onto the footpath and steps that take a circuitous route up the wooded hillside. Join a road and turn right, next to the railway track.

15' At a junction turn right, signed '*Plage Cenitz*'. Pass the Cenitz beach restaurant which is a great place to watch the sunset. Climb the hill using wooden steps onto the clifftop path where there is a panel about the Basques and the sea. Join a cycle route then go down steps to another beach. Cross the river on a footbridge, pass a helicopter pad and climb the hill ahead.

30' Join a road, walk up through a car park and across a roundabout and walk past camp sites and Mayarco beach.

40' Camping Playa Turn right after the campsite onto a footpath, cross a road and continue through the wooded escarpment above Laffitenia beach.

55' At the end of the beach, pass a car park and continue along the cliff top path. Turn left where the path is closed due to a rockfall. Join a road, turn right, and at the end of the road walk down to the beach at Erromardie.

I hr 10' Erromardie beach, water, toilets, refreshments, bus service. Walk along the sea front, join a cycle path and then climb through a car park and up the coastal path. At a road junction, by a toilet, turn right and go up to a cross on the edge of the cliff. Turn left along the cliff top, next to the fence of the Botanic Gardens.

View towards Biarritz

1 hr 40' Information panel at a high cliff top viewpoint. Turn left when the path is closed by another landslip and up the road ahead. Turn right at a junction, walk past the Reserve hotel, and then some blockhouses till you reach the lighthouse at St Barbe.

2hrs, St Barbe, headland overlooking the bay of St Jean de Luz. Go down to the esplanade and walk round the bay as far as the lighthouse at the far end of the beach. Just before the lighthouse, turn left off the sea wall and follow the road next to the port as far as:

2 hrs, 45' Place Louis XIV, St Jean de Luz

Beaches
Guéthary – popular with surfers
Cenitz – sand, pebbles and rock pools
Laffitenia – surf and sand
Erromardie – sand and rock pools
St Jean de Luz - sheltered sandy beach

25

9. Col des Trois Fontaines

This walk can be done using the bus service from St Jean de Luz. It is a circuit that goes high on the Rhune and includes a Napoleonic fort.

400m of ascent, 2hrs, 45'

ACCESS: Take the bus from St Jean de Luz or drive to the Col de St Ignace, from where the rack railway ascends the Rhune.

WALK

Col de St Ignace 169m - Walk up the road past the railway station and then cross the railway on a concrete track, through a picnic area. After 5' turn left at the large yellow arrows and cross back over the railway. The path turns W and crosses a stream before climbing onto the crest of a ridge.

15' - Turn left (signpost '*Sommet*') and SW on a track, climbing steadily and then passing a conifer plantation before turning right (signpost) on a footpath that climbs onto the ridge. Turn right to view the redoubt.

45' Napoleonic Redoubt 532m *0612268 4797122* This star shaped fort was used as a defensive position by the Napoleonic army retreating from the Peninsular war during the battle of the Rhune in 1813. The ridge ahead contains a line of further fortifications but the path turns right and W towards the sea to avoid the short climb.

1hr 5" Col des Trois Fontaines 532m A large grassy col. Turn right and cross a stream. Follow the red/white waymarks of the GR10 WNW. Walk next to a wood and up to a col.

1hr 20" Col, 562m *0610852 4796965* signpost. Turn right and NE on a path towards a stone refuge, a useful place to shelter or even stay overnight. The path soon descends and joins a larger trail, passing a chapel to the left. Turn right after a stand of conifers, as the path turns N and then E, before descending into a valley with a *bergerie.* 416m.

1hr 50' Join a stony track, turn left and N, cross a stream and descend towards Ascain. Pass a shelter on your left (120', 340m)

2hrs, 5' Take a shortcut to the right, leaving the large path and descending N through gorse. Briefly rejoin the stony track, stay right at a junction, cross another track and descend through trees to the road.

2hrs, 20" Car park 144m Walk down the road to the village, past the *restaurant des chasseurs* and the church.

2hrs, 45' Ascain - The bus stop is by the *fronton*.

It is also possible to descend from the Col des Trois Fontaines along the GR10 to the beautiful village of Sare, from where you can also catch the return bus.

Napoleonic Redoubt

The battle of the Rhune took place in November 1813. The allied army of English, Spanish, Portuguese and German troops were led by the Duke of Wellington, the French by Marechal Soult, whose 50,000 troops had to defend 50km of mountainous frontier. Fierce fighting and heavy casualties occurred before the French retreated towards the fortress at Bayonne and the allies occupied St Jean de Luz.

10. Atxuria

This route takes you over the rocky summit of Atxuria, down past prehistoric remains to Zugarramurdi, a village long associated with witchcraft. Return via ancient paths and among limestone caves once used by smugglers.
4 hours, 700m of ascent

ACCESS: Drive or take the bus to the Grottes de Sare

WALK
Grottes de Sare. Walk down the road from the cave entrance and after 50m turn left and through a gate on a path SW signed 'Venta Loretxoa' with green/pink marks.

10' The path joins a stony track; turn left and uphill, stay left at a junction and just before a *bergerie* turn left on the track, which goes up through gorse SSE onto the flank of the mountain.

30' join a dirt road and go up to the right. Stay right at a junction. Continue SW with the green/pink marks.

45' Col Akoka, 456m, *0615462 – 4790728* Venta Loretxoa Go through a gap in the fence and turn left and E along the ridge and through mature beech trees with the cliffs of the summit ridge above you to the left.

1hr 5' Shoulder of a ridge. Turn left following a yellow mark and climb up the grassy shoulder SSE on an indistinct path to the summit rocks. Walk with the rocks to your left until you come to a grassy gully marked by a cairn and a small tree. Climb the gully, and follow cairns to exit right near the top.

1 hr 35' Atxuria, 758m *0616107 – 4790208* Descend NE along the summit ridge towards the village of Zugarramurdi, following yellow marks. After 10' turn right at a large cairn, and then leave the yellow marks which go right and head SE down into the valley and towards the Col de Ibaineta.

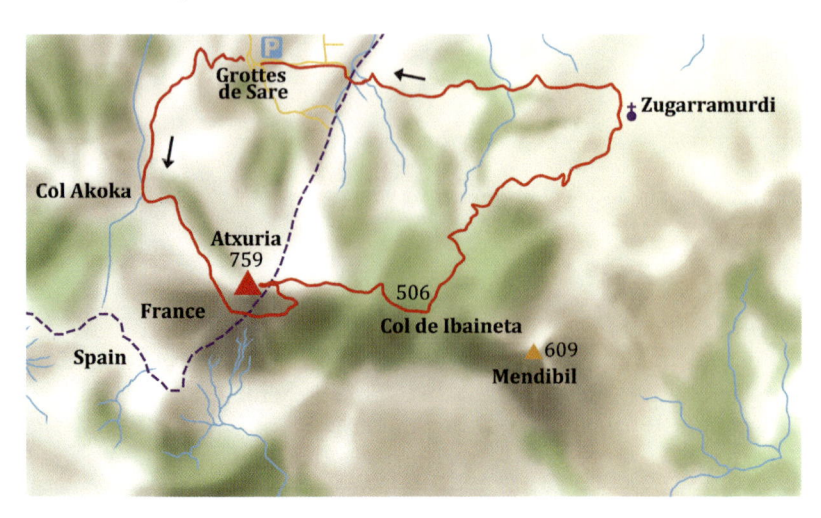

2hrs, Col de Ibaineta 514m, *0617239 – 4790147* stone circles and burial sites, signpost. Turn left and NE and descend through the forest following white/yellow marks. At a house, go down the road, and after 50m turn right on a track that crosses a stream. Continue steadily ENE through woods with fine views of the Rhune and the coast. The track widens and joins a river at a ruin. Cross the river and soon arrive at the village.

3hrs, Zugarramurdi village, restaurants.
Turn left at the church and follows signs to the caves. Walk past the witchcraft museum and the cave entrance. Then turn left following signs of a blue pony, which go back to the Grottes de Sare. Go down along the edge of a field, cross a river at a bridge and climb S. Join a road and turn right and NW.

3hrs, 40' Information stones. Leave the road and descend past limestone caves. Turn left at a house, then right down a road and immediately left at a junction. Take the path to the left of a road back to the Grottes de Sare.

4hrs, Grottes de Sare
If you wish to walk to Zugarramurdi without climbing the Atxuria then from the Grottes de Sare walk up through the quarry car park and onto a paved path to the right of the road. Follow the symbols of the blue pony as far as the village, using the previous instructions in reverse.

11. Alcurrunz

A fine rocky peak with stunning views and megalithic menhirs.
350m of ascent, 2 hours 30'

ACCESS: Follow the road from Dancheria towards Pamplona and 1/2km after the Otxondo pass you find a turn to the right and a car park with toilets and water. 600m

WALK
Walk SW along the road and after 10' a farm track joins from the left.

10' Signpost 'Alcurrunz'. Climb up the grassy ridge towards the summit leaving a horizontal stone cross to your right. Follow the green & white waymarks as the ridge becomes rocky.

45' Col, 764m. Standing menhirs. Follow the waymarks west initially as the path flanks the side of the summit.

70' Col. Turn N back up the grassy slope towards the summit. Take the steps up the summit rocks past old fortifications and solar panels. A tunnel provides access to an underground fort.

90' Alcurrunz 934m *0621230 4786386* - Large cairn with message box. Retrace your steps to return in one hour.

2hrs, 30' Return to starting point

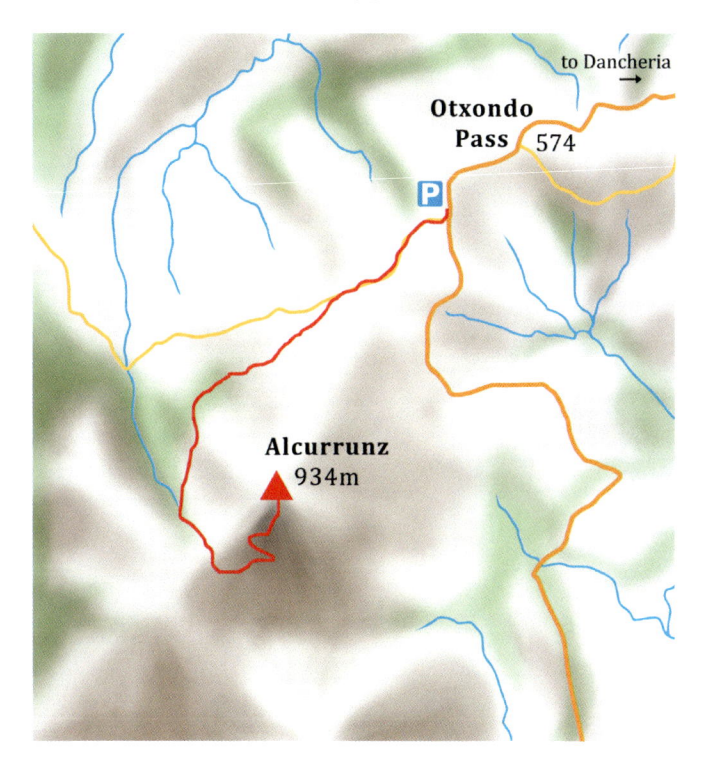

12. Mondarrain

A pleasant walk, which can easily be extended onto the Gorospil ridge to the South.

3 hours 30', 400m of ascent

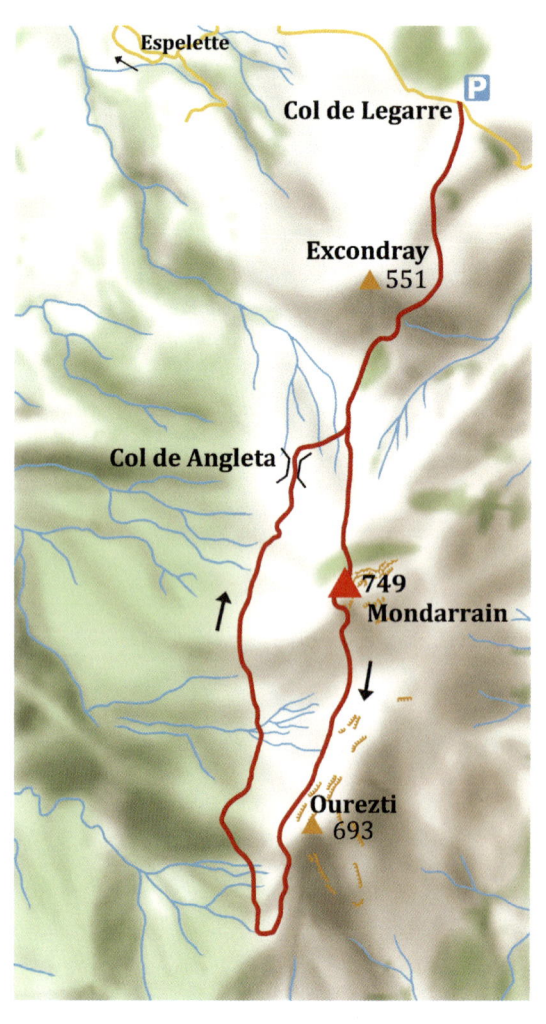

ACCESS: start from the Col de Legarre. Take the D249 from Espelette towards Itxassou.

After 3 Km turn right at a small *col* (signpost 'Mondarrain').

The road climbs steeply for 2km more up to a col with a house on either side of the road.

Park beside the road just after the Col de Legarre (350m).

WALK
From the *col* a large path goes SW and the rocky summit soon comes into view.

Leave a conifer plantation (30') to your left and go down beside it and then up S on the clearly marked path towards the summit. A beech forest surrounds the rocky summit. Follow the yellow marks initially SW through the granite blocks and then turn S and up and around the summit to avoid the larger cliffs.

I hr 30' Mondarrain. The cross on the summit sits above the remains of a 12th century fortified tower. To descend, continue S following the yellow waymarks on a path which passes the near the broken summit ridge of Mt Ourezti (693m).

2hrs, Ourezti Continue S and pass a stone circle on your left before arriving at a small *col* just before a hillock.

2hrs, 30' Col – Turn right on a track to the N which contours back round the side of Mondarrain.

3hrs, Col de Angleta - Take the track down towards the plantation you passed earlier and retrace your steps back to the start.

3hrs, 30' Return to the start

13. Ursuya

Ursuya is of modest altitude but standing apart from the rest of the Basque hills it is a great belvedere for the mountains all the way from the coast to the high Pyrenees.

400m of ascent, 3 hours

ACCESS: From the village of Mendionde, drive up past the church and continue for 1km and park at a *col* with a signpost '*Urtsuko itzulia*'. 274m, *0637358 4801076*.

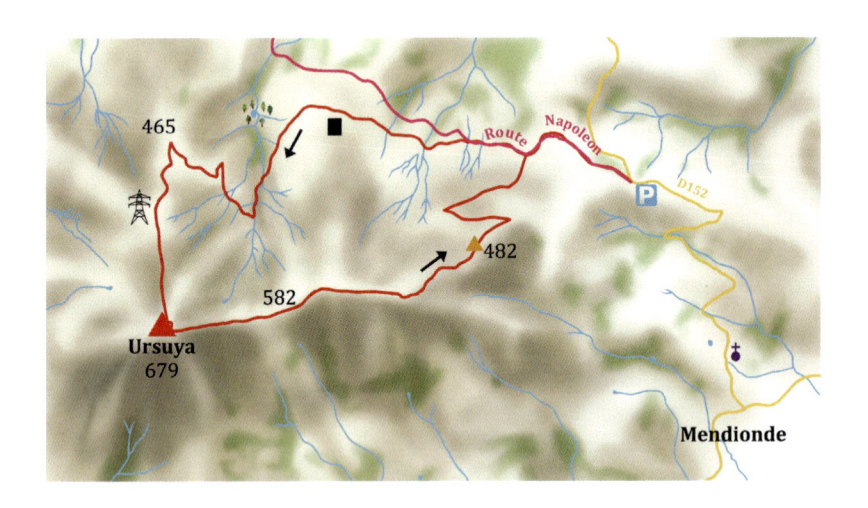

WALK

Take the track NW, you are walking on the 'Route Napoleon' built to move troops quickly from the coast inland during. Follow the yellow marks. After 10' go straight over at a crossroads, soon after the track turns right and you a join a road with a cattle grid. Pass a house and after 15' leave the Route Napoleon near a sign erected by the commune of Hasparran and take a track that rises west. Leave the yellow marks. Cross a stream.

30' *Bergerie* 364m The track levels off. Descend past a well-built *bergerie* and a Hasparran drinking water sign. Cross the wooded streambed by fenced off water collection points and climb up to the ridge ahead, at first straight, then flank right.

55' Ridge, ruin, 471m Turn left and climb up the ridge SSW on an indistinct path.

1 hr 15' Antenna, 584m Join a larger path and continue up the ridge, past a subsidiary summit 656m.

1 hr 30' Mt Ursuya, 678m, cairn, trig point, panoramic views. Descend on the ridge to the east. After 30 metres drop down SE to join the path that follows the ridge E.

2hrs, summit, 595m Continue to descend E on a large path towards the village of Mendionde. Continue E on the ridge when the trail goes right past a small plantation.

2hrs, 15' *col* before a bump on the ridge, 475m. Go down left NNE at first , then NW through a grassy field to join a sandy farm track. Turn right (E) onto the track.

2hrs, 40' Gate, continue and soon follow the track left, next to a line of fencing. At a crossroads (305m) turn right, you are back on the Route Napoleon.

3hrs, Return to the start.

14. Gorospil Cirque

Walk on the ridges above the magnificent fortified village of Ainhoa.
750m of ascent, 5 hours 30'

ACCESS: From Ainhoa take the road towards Dancharia and after 2km turn left onto a side road (signed 'ventas') and park after 600m at a *col*, just before a quarry. 130m (*0622166 – 4794135*)

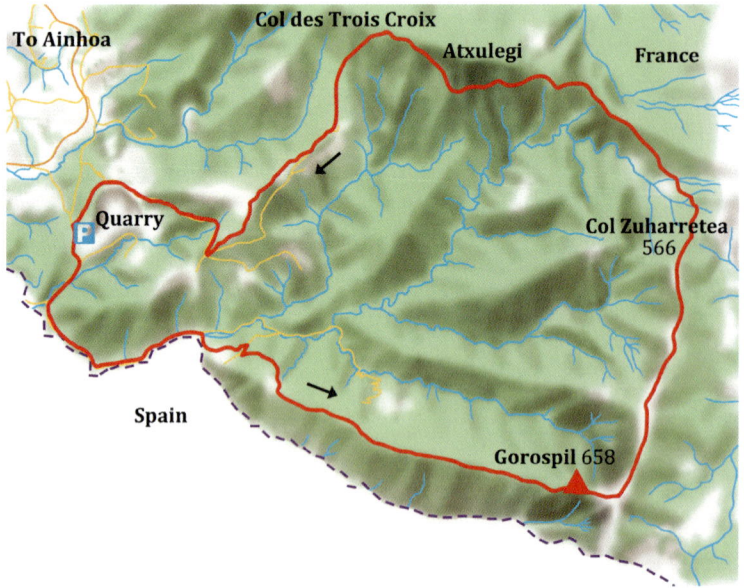

WALK
Walk down the tarmac past the quarry entrance. After 10' cross a cattle grid where the road turns SSE and then ENE following a river which marks the frontier.

30' Footbridge Cross the river just before a fish farm. Climb SSE through the forest following yellow marks; join a road for 100m before continuing in the forest until you come to a *col*.

1hr Col - Leave the yellow marks and head SE up the ridge where the view soon opens towards Mt Gorospil. At the end of the ridge climb steeply up grass to the summit.

2hrs, 15' Mt Gorospil, 691m, grassy mound with marker stone. *0626145 – 4792265* Turn NE along the ridge. Go over a summit but leave the ridge just before the final summit and cut down NNE towards the Col de Zuharretea.

2hrs, 50' Col de Zuharretea 566m. Join the red and white markings of the GR10 and go down N past a stand of mature beech trees and several *bergeries*.

3hrs, 20' junction of tracks, 430m. You can continue on the GR10 which climbs W on the large track which flanks the side of Mt Atxulegi. In good weather climb the ridge directly over the summit to enjoy the views to the north and pass an area popular with vultures.

4hrs, Col des Trois Croix, 513m. Only one cross can be seen. Leave the GR and turn left WSW down a track. At a col (355m), join a small road and follow it SW next to telephone poles. After 200m leave the road on a small path and pass a house on your left as you continue along the ridge which undulates over two high points (386m and 383m) before dropping down and rejoining the road at a junction.

5hrs, road junction 302m. Turn right and N on the tarmac and descend with views of the quarry.

5hrs, 30' Return to the starting point.

15. Baigora

Walk up the long southern ridge of the Baigora, a mountain whose position a little apart from the main ranges provides an excellent panoramic viewpoint.

800m of ascent, 6 hours

ACCESS: Start in the village of Osses. If travelling on the D918 from Cambo to St Jean Pied de Port, turn left once in Osses, signed 'centre bourg'.

After 1 km, just before a red stone church and a fronton, turn left towards 'Ecole St Michel', on a road with yellow marks.

At a junction turn left then right by a signpost 'Haltzamendi'.

The road ends at a farm. 139m *0638518 – 4789578* Park just before the farm.

WALK

Climb past the farm NW on the stony track following yellow marks. After 10' turn right NE past a barn and then N up onto the ridge on the well-marked path among chestnut trees.

45' *Bergerie*. Come out of the trees, and leave the *bergerie* on your right, then turn right NE along the ridge. Pass a signpost (550m) as the path turns towards the NW.

1hr 15' junction 600m, stay left and then traverse horizontally at first, before descending slightly to a signpost 575m on the shoulder of a ridge. Turn right N and continue up the left side of the ridge.

2hrs, junction - Signpost 'Haltzamendi' 722m *0637467 - 4792508* - Baigora with summit antennae comes into view. Optionally climb E to the summit of Haltzamendi and back. Continue horizontally N.

2hrs, 30' 752m - A band of rock sits across the ridge. This can be avoided by following the yellow posts over to the right (E) side of the ridge and taking care not to drop too low before returning to the ridge. It is also possible to clamber across the rocks along the ridge via an indistinct path.

2hrs, 45' Rejoin the ridge, and continue N leaving the summit of Mt Laina to your right. After a *col* climb to the summit.

3hrs, 30' Baigora, 897m *0638479 – 4794481* - Popular with parachutists. Return by the same route.

6hrs, Return to the start.

16. Ichusi

From the beautiful Baztan valley over the summit of Ichusi and then along the top of the spectacular cliffs with their vultures. Return via the col and cromlechs at Méhatche.
4hrs, 45', 600m of ascent

ACCESS: Cross the River Nive at Pont Noblia. Don't go up to Bidarray but turn right and then right again at a bridge crossing the river Baztan. Stay left and go up the road next to the river. After the road crosses the river for the first time the red/white GR10 markings appear. The road eventually climbs steeply and ends at a farm after 3km. Park just before the farm. 274m, *0631106 – 4791304*

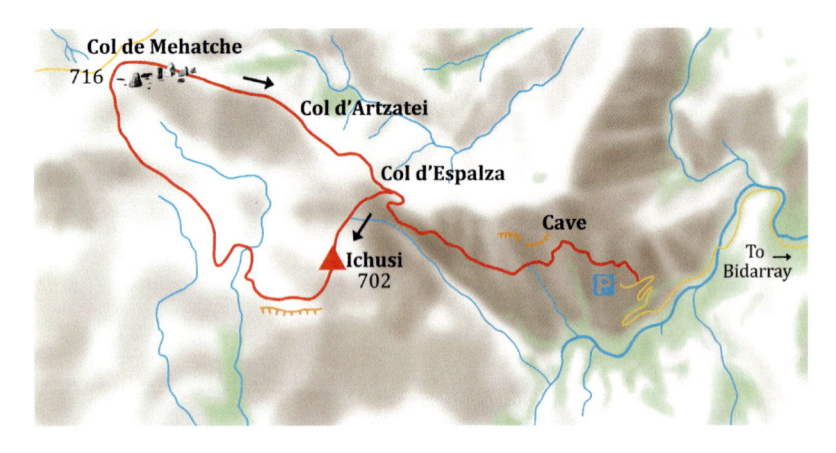

WALK
The GR10 climbs on a path N and after 20' reaches the cave of the Saint qui Sue (*0630723 – 4791507*). The saint is represented by a stalagmite and the water is believed to heal skin conditions. Continue NW along the ever steepening side of a ravine. Cross patches of scree as the path steepens and cables are provided for protection. This is rough terrain and best avoided if wet. Just before the *col* a narrow path leading SSW

goes towards the Ichusi cliffs. Stay on the GR and arrive at the Col de Espalza.

1 hr, 20' Col de Espalza, 642m, signpost *0629898 – 4791753* Leave the GR and climb SW up the gentle grassy slope over a rise and onto the summit of Ichusi.

1hr, 40' Ichusi, 702m Continue S past a marker stone until you reach a path coming from the left. Turn right and follow this west and just above a line of spectacular cliffs with views of vultures.

2hrs, 10' Cross the Ezpaiza stream, 543m *0629188 – 4791169* just before it plunges over the cliffs. Climb up past a shelter and ruin and then climb N away from the cliffs over a high point (626m) and towards the radars on the summit of Artzamendi. The path turns NW past a small col and traverses NNW towards the Col de Méhatche.

2hrs, 50' Col de Méhatche, 716m, frontier stone 80 near a menhir. *0628494 – 4792307* Take the GR10 SSE but after 100m climb N 50m to see the fine stone circles (*0628770 – 4792404).* Return to the GR10 and follow the grassy ridge SSE past frontier stone 82 next to a huge rock which is a fallen menhir.

3hrs, 25' Col d'Artzatei, Frontier stone 83. Stay on the left side of the ridge to skirt the next rise until you reach the Col de Espalza.

3hrs, 35' Col de Espalza. Retrace your steps by dropping steeply into the ravine and back towards the start.

4hrs, 45' Return to the start.

17. Mt Larla Mining circuit

A high level circumnavigation of Mt Larla, the most important iron age mining area in the Basque country. More than 20 centuries of mining activity have left their mark on the mountain where open and subterranean mines, Roman workshops, and an aerial transporter can be seen.
550m of ascent, 4 hours 30'

ACCESS: From the fronton in St Martin d'Arrosa, take the road W signed 'Satali'. Climb steeply and after 2km the car park on the right of the road at Satali has an info panel about the walk.

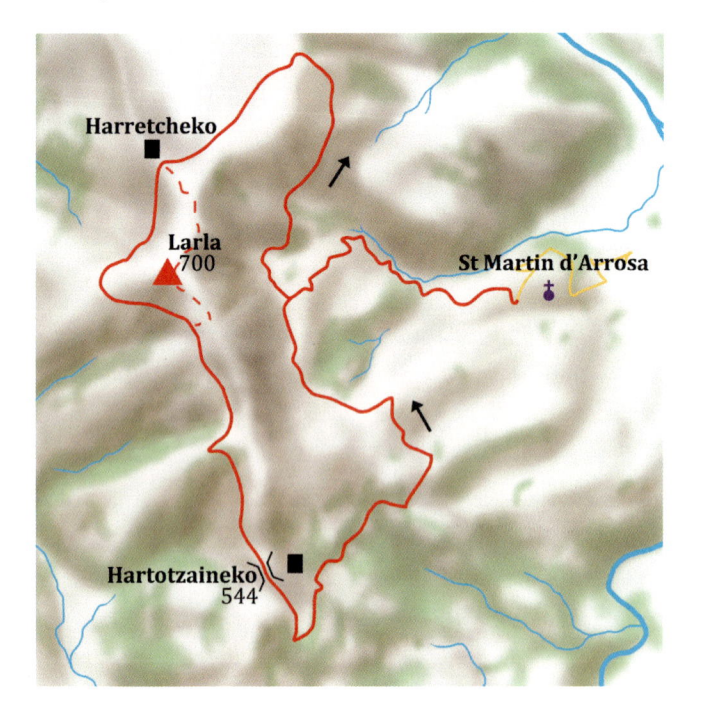

WALK
Satali 236m *0621891 – 4787802* Continue along the road following the red marks that will guide you today. After 10' turn left and SW on a stony track just before a *bergerie*. Climb past mine workings; at a junction turn right then left through a

gate and climb NW. After 30' pass an information panel and come to a grassy col.

50' Col Turn right and then up across grass to join a dirt road which goes SW to flank the side of Mt Larla.

1hr 25' Col, Harretchecko Borda, *bergerie* 624m, info panel - The highest point of the walk with great views of the Iparla Crêtes. (On a clear day it is worth the detour up to the summit from here for the fine 360° views.) Descend slightly then continue on the more or less horizontal path that flanks around Mt Larla. Pass an information panel before the path turns to the E. There are traces of mining activity as the path narrows and crosses steep terrain.

2hrs, 45' *Col.* **Harotzaineko Borda** 540m. Info panel. Descend SE then after 15' turn sharply NE at a *bergerie* in a wood. Go through forest on an undulating path back towards the start.

3hrs, 25' After crossing a ridge climb W towards Mt Larla.

3hrs, 40' *Col* 502m. The highest point of the return. Continue W past mine workings and info panels.

4hrs, 10' Rejoin the outward path at the first info panel and retrace your steps to the start point.

4hrs, 30' Satali

18. Crêtes d'Iparla from Urdos

Up through woods to the impressive frontier ridge of the Crêtes d'Iparla.
4 hours 45', 800m of ascent

ACCESS: Turn right off the road from Cambo to Saint-Étienne-de-Baïgorry to the hamlet of Urdos. Park in the centre, near a large stone residence (once a hunting lodge).

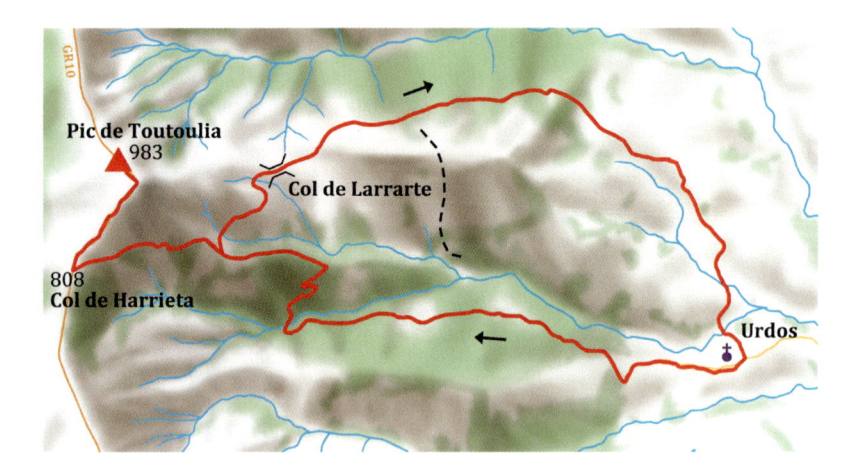

WALK
Take the track to the right of the residence, signed towards the Col de Larrarte. Follow the yellow marks west up the large track that climbs the wooded Urdos valley, with the river below to your right. Stay right at a junction after 20' when the gradient eases and again after 30' just before a *bergerie*.

40' Cross a stream; the track then climbs onto the crest of a ridge.

60' Bergerie Sarrasare, junction with signpost, pointing towards the col de Larrarte that you will use for the descent. Continue climbing past the bergerie through mature beech woods, to the Col de Harrieta.

1hr 30' Col de Harrieta 808m signpost. Follow the red/white marks of the GR10 N to the summit.

2hrs, 5' Toutoulia, 983m *0631463 4786016*, marked by feeble cairn. Views along the crêtes. Return the way you came to the *bergerie* and then turn left to the Col de Zarrarte.

3hrs, 5' Col de Zarrarte - Continue E on the obvious track, with great views of the Crêtes d'Iparla, past a couple of ruins and descending steadily.

3hrs, 45' Signpost 'Urdos' - The track turns to the left. Leave the track and follow the footpath E, above a green valley, using the yellow marks.

4hrs, 10' At an intersection, by a *bergerie*, turn left and walk towards the village. Briefly join a road and then turn right by some barns onto a footpath (signpost). Cross a junction, then two streams before climbing up to Urdos.

4hrs, 45' Urdos.

19. Iparla from Ispeguey

From the Col d'Ispeguey. A classic ridge walk. Well-organised parties can arrange to leave a car at Bidarray and walk the whole ridge.
1100m of ascent, 6 hours, 15'

ACCESS: Drive to the Col d'Ispeguey from Saint-Étienne-de-Baïgorry in France or Arizcun in Spain.

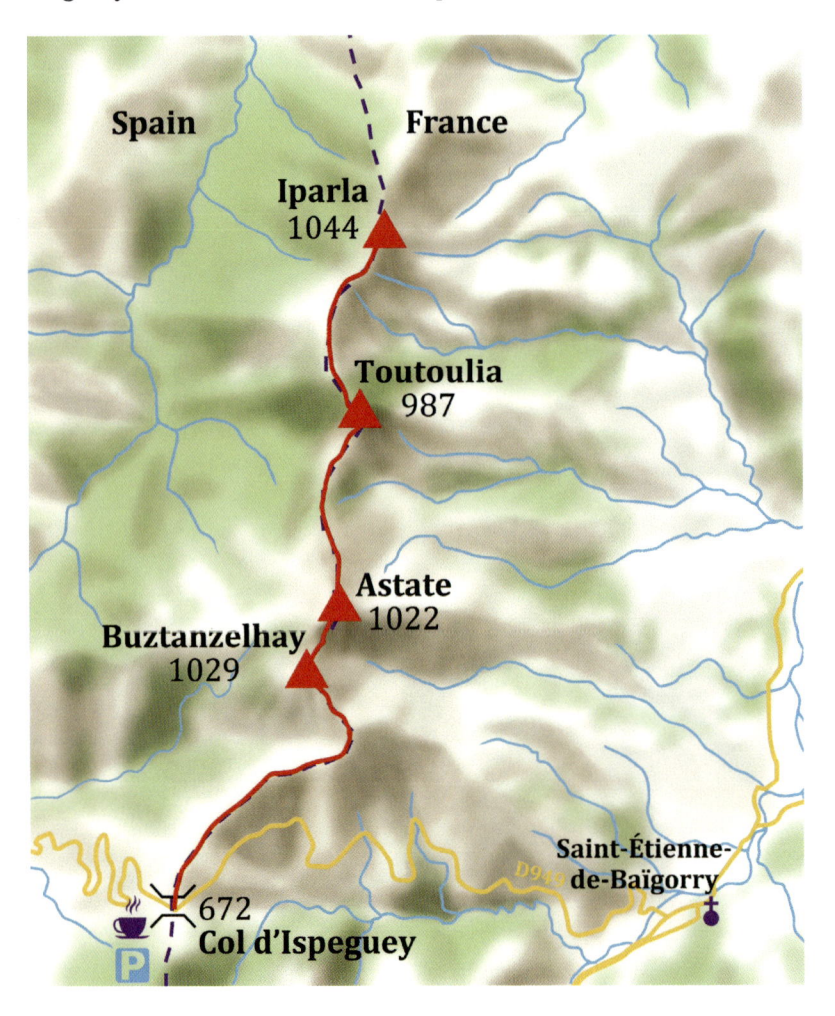

WALK

Col d'Ispeguey, 672m, restaurant - Walk up the ridge NE next to conifers, following the red/white marks that will guide you all day. After a short climb the path levels off on the left side of the ridge.

45' Col d'Aintziaga, cairn, 776m Cross to the SE side of the ridge.

55' Cross back over the NW side of the ridge, by beech trees. Pass a small stream and head N towards the col and summit of Butzanzelhay.

1hr 5' Col de Butzanzelhay, 820m, signpost. The GR10 comes up from Baigorry to the right. Continue NW up the ridge ahead. The path climbs round the side of the ridge before approaching the summit from the West.

1hr 30' Butzanzelhay, cairn, 1029m *0631089 4783662* Continue NNE along the path next to the cliff edge.

1hr 40' Col de Astate, 957m, dolmen - Climb the rocky section of the ridge ahead with the help of cairns before continuing on the cliff edge path.

1hr 50' Astate, 1022m Continue along the ridge and then descend past blocks of *poudding* and into the beech woods at the Col de Harrieta.

2hrs, 10' Col de Harrieta, 808m, water source in woods 400m S of col, signposted from the GR. Continue N up the ridge.

2hrs, 45' Toutoulia, 983m 0631463 4786016, marked by feeble cairn. Continue NNW as the ridge becomes rockier.

3hrs, 15' Iparla, 1040m, concrete pillar.
Retrace your steps to return in 3 hours to Ispeguey.

The Iparla ridge is one of the finest days on the long distance GR10 and you are likely to encounter walkers, some of whom are hoping to walk a further 40 days to the Mediterranean. Accommodation is provided for walkers in
Saint-Étienne-de-Baïgorry at the Gîte Gaineko Karrikan (+33 5 59 37 47 04). This is also the centre of the Iroulegey wine region.

20. Hautza

From the Col d'Ispeguey
First summit over 1300m inland from the coast. Panoramic views and extensive iron age site.
650m of ascent, 5 hours

ACCESS: Drive to the Col d'Ispeguey from Saint-Étienne-de-Baïgorry in France or Arizcun in Spain.

WALK
Col d'Ispeguey 672m - From the car park take the path that drops slightly to the south. Signpost 'Elorrieta'. Follow the red/white waymarks along the track which soon narrows to a path that climbs gently through beautiful beech woods.

40' The path comes out of the woods and turns SW towards the summit.

55' Col de Nekaitzeko, 814m, stone-walled enclosure, line of shooting posts. Continue SW, past a *bergerie*.

1hr 10' Col d'Elorrieta, 831m, frontier stone 102, iron age burial sites 50m to the left, with info panel. 0629474 4779321 Climb the frontier ridge SSW into the forest, following red/white marks past blocks of *poudding.*

1hr 55' small col, 118m The path straight up to the summit is steep and stony. Instead, continue SW on a path that rises slightly and crosses an eroded slope to reach the ridge that runs between Hautza and Antchola (2hrs, 10'). Then follow cairns NW to the summit.

2hrs, 40' Hautza, 1306m, concrete pillar, memorials. Views over the valleys of Baztan and Aldudes and to the coast.
Return the same way in 2hrs, 20'. 5 hours, in total.

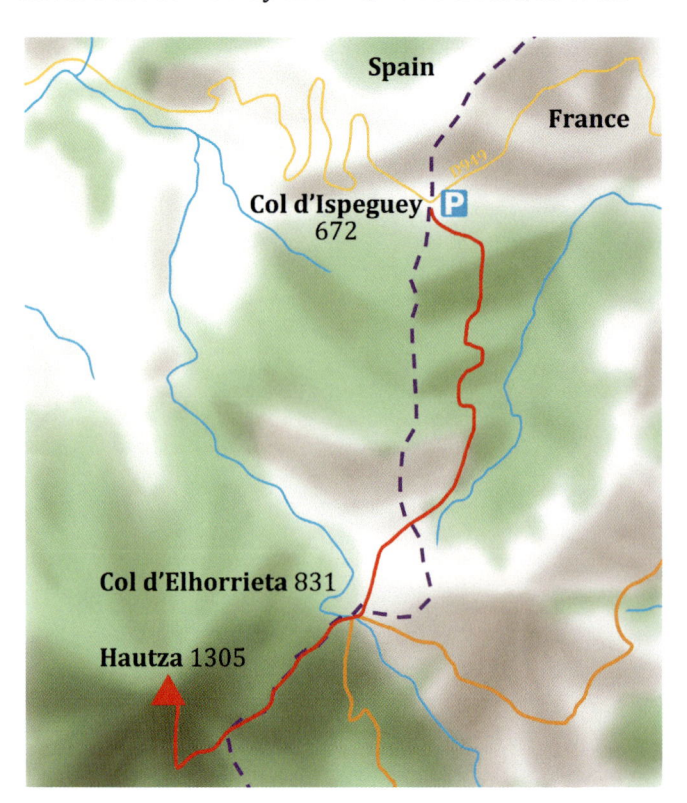

21. Harguibel

The remote valley of Aldudes is a lovely place to spend some time, known for its good food, rare breed pigs and trout farms.
800m of ascent, 4 hours 45'

ACCESS: Park in the village of Aldudes, near the church. There is an information panel with a map of this walk.

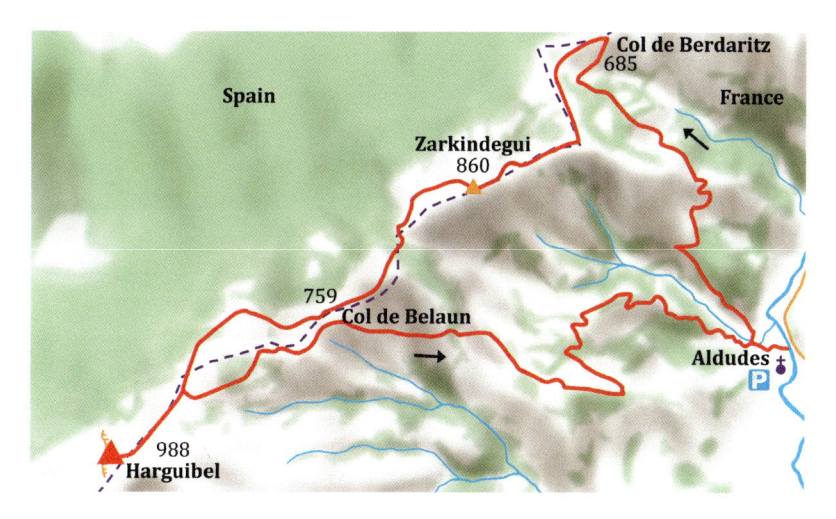

WALK
Aldudes 355m Walk west on a road with the yellow waymarks that you will follow today. At a signpost, '*Hargibel*', turn right across a stream and then steeply up the road. After 15' the road ends. Continue on the track that zigzags up the hill towards the NW. After 35' the track levels off and goes through beech woods.

1hr Col de Berdaritz, 685m, Frontier Stone (FS) 117, *0627000 4774450* Turn left WSW on a grassy path up the frontier ridge into woods. Soon fork left and SW at a junction, 725m. Come out of the woods and turn S.

1hr 25' FS 119, signpost '*Hargibel*' - Turn W and climb to the summit of Zarkindegui.

1hr 40' Zarkindegui 860m FS 121, 0626566 4773708 Continue W on the right side of ridge, then descend SW into woods.

2hrs, 10' Col de Belaun 758m You can turn left here to pick up the return path if you wish to shorten the walk. Continue SW on the ridge.

2hrs, 30' *Col*, 846m, FS 125 Climb SW to the rocky summit of Harguibel.

2hrs, 50' Harguibel 988m The summit rocks can be climbed by an airy scramble via the obvious gap to the right. To extend the walk continue on the path that leads to the summit of Peña de Alba. To return, descend to the *col* and go down the road which soon turns east. At the next bend turn left onto a path NE into the woods. Signed '*Aldudes*'.

3hrs, 25' Col de Belaun - Continue descending on the track ENE.

3hrs, 40' Join a road and turn left, 646m. The road soon turns SE past a line of shooting posts. At a junction turn left. The road climbs slightly and winds past a couple of streams.

4hrs, 15' The road ends at a farm 'Elokadi Alde', 572m. Turn right onto a track NE. Join another road and descend to the village.

4hrs, 45' Aldudes

22. Monhoa

Great views over the valleys of St Jean Pied de Port and Aldudes make this worth doing on a clear day. Easy navigation on the well-marked GR10.
900m of ascent, 5 hours

ACCESS: Take the turn off to the village of Lasse from the St Jean Pied de Port to Saint-Étienne-de-Baïgorry road. From Lasse drive 2 km uphill on small roads marked with the red/white GR waymarks. Park at a wide junction, near a barn. *0639527 4779570,* 319m.

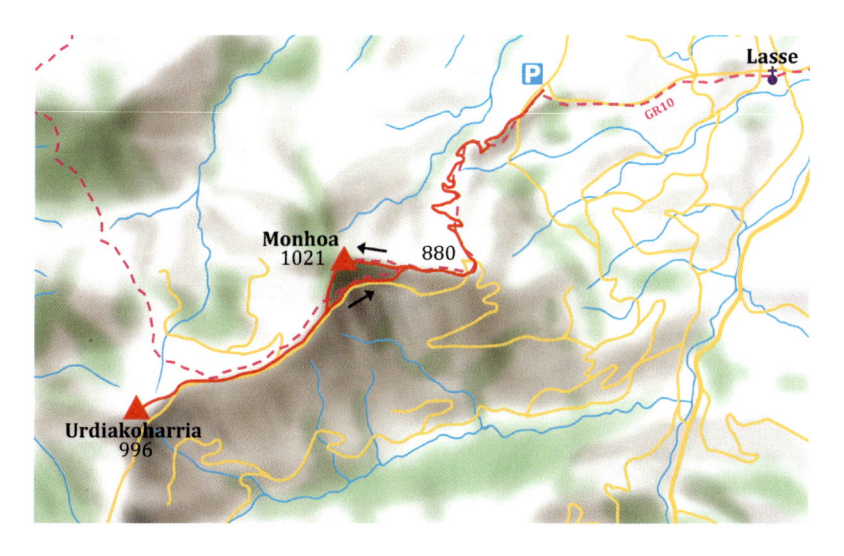

WALK
Turn left and walk up the dirt road SW towards the grassy mountain ahead, the Monhoa. Look for the red/white waymarks of the GR10 that will guide you today. After 10' turn right and WSW onto a track by a signpost '*Monhoa*'. Zigzag up the grassy slope ahead. Various shortcuts are possible.

1hr 15' Join the ridge, by a road. 744m. Water point. Cross the road and climb the ridge W.

1hr 45' 875m Briefly join a road at a water tank. Continue W up steep grass to the summit.

2hrs, Monhoa, 1021m 0624181 4802161, antenna. Go down the grassy ridge SW following the red/white waymarks.

2hrs, 20' Col d'Urdanzia 872m road junction with cross and *bergerie.* Continue WSW on or near the road. At a junction (920m) the GR10 descends on a path to the right. Stay on the road, and then climb right to the summit.

2hrs, 50' Urdiakoharria, 996m, cross. View into the valley of Aldudes.

Return by the same way though you can skirt round the summit of Monhoa by walking on the small road, past a water point. 2 hours to return, a little under 5 hours in all.

23. Occabe

You will enjoy walking in Iraty, the largest deciduous forest in Europe and visiting the most important megalithic site in the eastern Basque country.
600m of ascent, 3 hours 45'

ACCESS: Start at Chalet Pedro, 1km south of the junction of the D18 and D301.

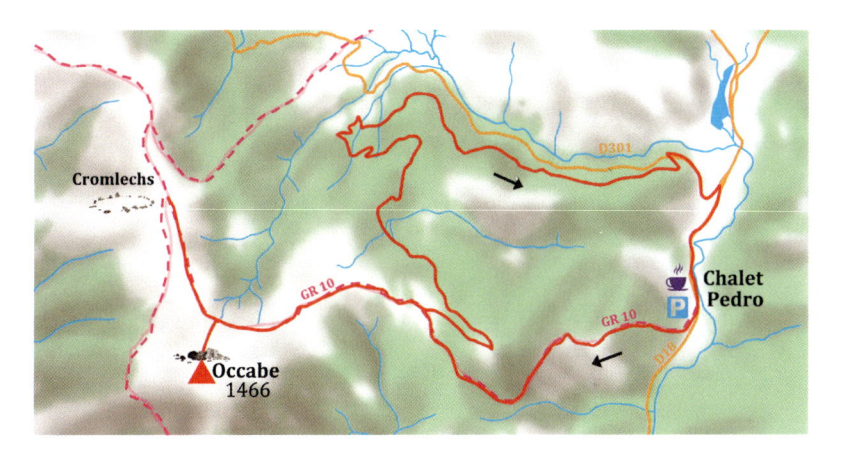

WALK
Chalet Pedro, 1000m Walk S on the road for 50m and turn right on a path with red/white waymarks that winds its way WSW up the forest. You are walking on the GR10.

15' The path comes out of the forest and continues next to it, at first W, then SW.

45' junction in heather, signpost 'OKABE" 1305m Continue W, you will use the path going right for the descent.

50' Turn left at a junction and climb left past a large cairn, 1326m

1hr The GR by-passes the summit of Occabe. Turn left off the GR by a GR10 milestone and climb SW over grass and past rocks to the summit.

1 hr 25' Occabe, 1456m, extensive views. The cromlechs are on the grassy ridge to the north. Rejoin the GR before you get there.

1hr 45' Cromlechs d'Occabe, 1374m stone circles. Return the same way, but stay on the GR to pass the summit of Okabe.

2hrs, 15' junction in clearing with heather, to enjoy a longer walk in the forest, turn left by the signpost 'Iraty'. The path climbs slightly E through beautiful woodland, following yellow mountain bike marks.

2hrs, 25' The path turns left and back on itself. Descend NW on a winding forest track. Stay left at a couple of junctions.

3hrs, junction, with signpost 'IRATY". Turn right onto the forest trail that follows the contours east.

3 hrs, 30' The trail turns left and zigzags down to the road.

3hrs, 45' Walk along the road to Chalet Pedro. Accommodation and refreshments are available. (chaletpedro.com)

There are 26 stone circles at Occabe. They contain ashes at the centre and were used as burial sites. These and many other stone circles in the Basque country are in imposing positions, often near transhumance routes. The stone circles are frequently found in clusters, though no other site in the region has as many circles as Occabe. The stones were transported here but it is not known how.

24. Escaliers – Arthanolatze

A short walk onto a ridge with two summits that are both magnificent viewpoints.
520m of ascent, 2 hours 45'

ACCESS: From Col de Bagargiak (Chalets d'Iraty) 1327m
Chalets d'Iraty provide bunkhouse accommodation or you can rent a chalet. Tel 0559285586

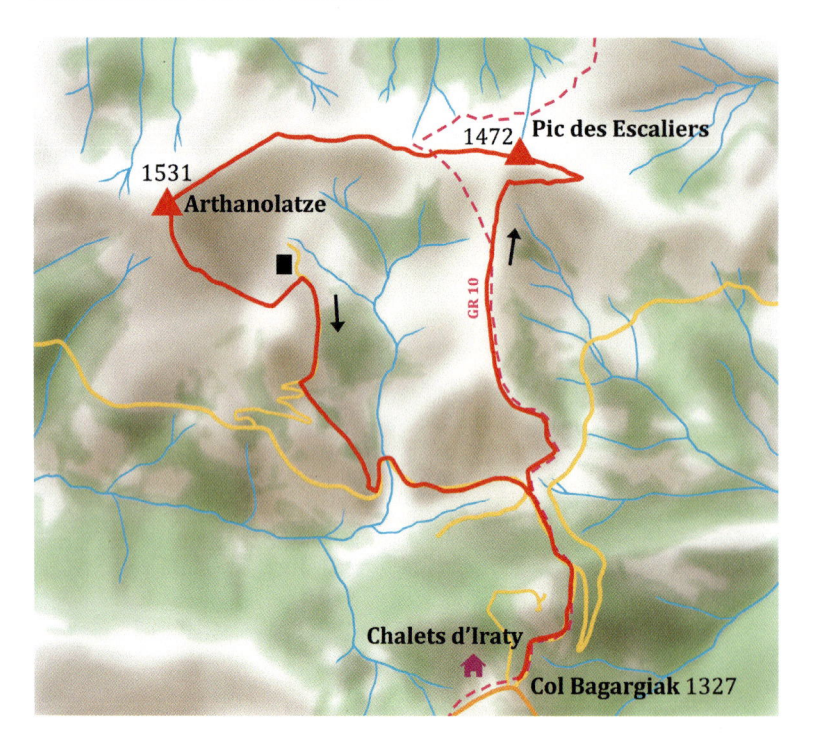

WALK
Start near the restaurant at the Chalets d'Iraty. Leave it to your left and walk down a road NE guided by the yellow marks you will follow today. Note also the red/white marks of the GR10

that you will follow for a short while. At a junction stay left, you soon arrive at the Col d'Iraitzabaleta.

10' Col d'Iraitzabaleta, 1254m, shooting posts. Go up the grassy path N. A zigzag takes you up onto the ridge.

30' ridge 1390m Continue N on the ridge towards the grassy summit of Escaliers. The GR soon turns left and follows the contour. Continue up the grassy slope following the yellow marks. The path traverses right just before the summit ridge, which it reaches at a subsidiary summit 1460m. Turn left and climb to the summit.

1hr Pic des Escaliers 1472m 0660801 – 4768664
Descend N on the ridge to a small col where you cross the GR, before climbing to the next summit.

1hr 30' Arthanolatze 1531m Turn left and descend the slope S towards Mt Orhy. At a small *col* turn left before a rocky outcrop and go down past a *bergerie* to a dirt road. Go down the road until it makes a couple of sharp turns, and then turn left and down through woods and gorse until you join the road again (1222m). Turn left and walk back to the Col d'Iraitzabaleta and retrace your steps on the road back to the restaurant, or go through the woods past the chalets.

2hrs, 45' Return to the start.

25. Pic d'Orhy

The highest summit entirely in the Basque country and much higher than anything nearby. The views are extensive but it is also prone to strong winds. Today you are walking on the Pyrenean Haute Route, there are no paint marks and only a few cairns to guide you. The route contains a section of exposed ridge and should only be done in good conditions.
800m of ascent, 4 hours 30'

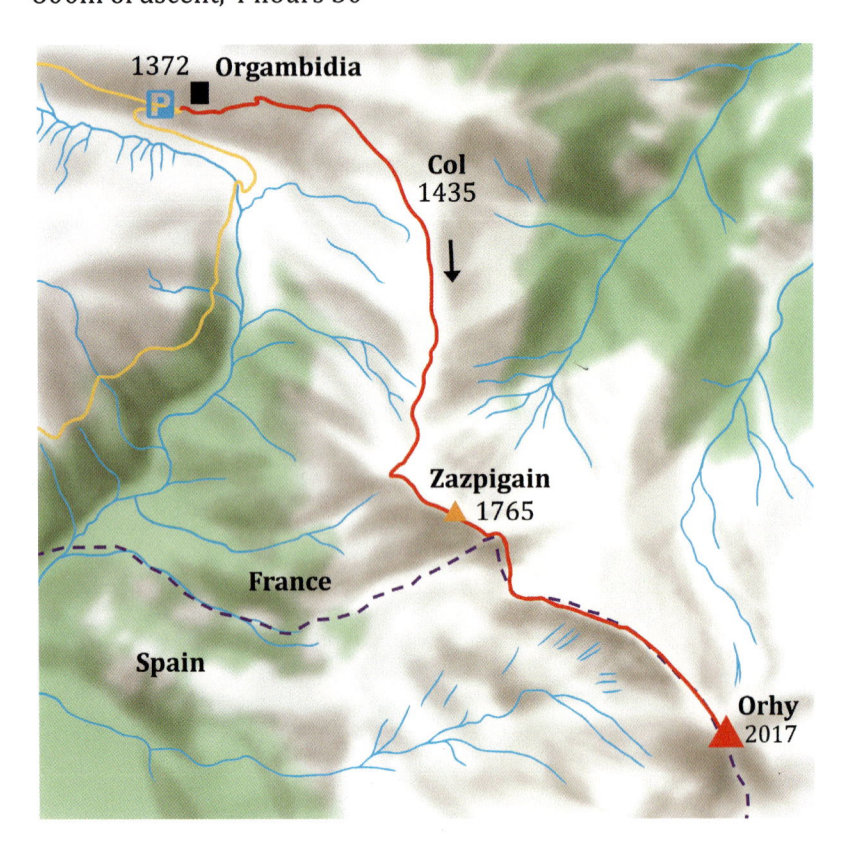

ACCESS: Start from Cayola d'Orgambida. Drive up the road behind the Chalets d'Iraty admin office. After 5km you come to the Col Leherra Murkhuillako. Descend a further 1km and the

Cayola d'Orgambida is the first *bergerie* on your left, by a sharp bend.

WALK
Cayola d'Orgambida 1372m *0660494 4763663* Walk E on a track past the bergerie. After 50m, by a tree, various sheep tracks going SE tempt you to avoid a small climb, but it is probably just as easy to stay on the track. In either case join the ridge at a col (1435m) and then walk up the ridge SE past a line of shooting posts. The ridge gets steep and rocky near the top and the path goes first right, then left on a ridge up to the summit of Zazpigain.

1hr 15' Zazpigain, 1765m, *0661545 4762257* - The ridge becomes narrow, rocky and increasingly exposed as you descend. Leave the ridge at a gap marked by a cairn *0661689 4762098* just before a rocky section and descend left 30m on the French side of the ridge, before climbing back to the ridge after the difficult section, using cables for protection in the final ascent. Climb up to the summit staying just to the right of the ridge.

2hrs, 30' Pic d'Orhy 2017m *0662549 4761475*, concrete pillar.

Return the same way in 2 hours.

Published by E-Publications 2016

Copyright © 2016 by Stephen Chadwick
All rights reserved. This book or any portion thereof may not be reproduced or used in any manner whatsoever without the written permission of the publisher.
First Printing, 2016
ISBN-13: 978-1518707810
E-Publications
49 Harvey Goodwin Ave
Cambridge CB4 3EX
www.basquewalks.com

Acknowledgements
Maps by Wainwright Illustration www.sophiewainwright.co.uk
Thanks to Dominique Chadwick for being a great walking companion. Also Patxi Veyret for advice on Mt Larla walk.

Disclaimer
All routes have been walked and described by Stephen Chadwick. Every effort has been made to make this book as accurate as possible. However, there may be typographical and or content errors. Therefore, this book should serve only as a general guide and not as the ultimate source of information. The author and publisher shall have no liability or responsibility to any person regarding any loss or damage incurred, directly or indirectly, by the information contained in this book.

Printed in Poland
by Amazon Fulfillment
Poland Sp. z o.o., Wrocław